Beautiful Soul

"The Life and Death of Esroy George Rowe"

EILEEN CARTER -BROWN

Beautiful Soul- The Life and Death of Esroy George Rowe
Copyright © July 2017 by
Eileen Carter- Brown.
Published in the United States of America by Gospel 4 U Publishing

www.gospel4unetwork.com

All rights reserved. No part of this book may be reproduced or transmitted in anyway by means, electronic, mechanical, Photocopy, recording or otherwise, without prior permission of the author except as provided by USA copyright law.

Scriptures are taken from the
Holy Bible unless otherwise marked.
ISBN - 9780998466514
Library of Congress Number - 2016962587

Printed in United States of America
July 2017

DEDICATION

ACKNOWLEDGEMENT

INTRODUCTION

FOREWORD

Chapter 1 11

Chapter 2 17

Chapter 3 25

Chapter 4 35

Chapter 5 45

Chapter 6 53

Chapter 7 63

LIFE GOES ON 69

LETTERS 71

POEMS 89

GALLERY OF LOVE 101

WORDS OF ENCOURAGEMENT 121

ABOUT THE AUTHOR

Dedication

In loving memory of my son, Esroy who was also affectionately known as "*Greg.*" who loved, laughed, and lived while touching so many lives, during his time here on Earth. We will forever keep your memories alive.

BEAUTIFUL SOUL

Acknowledgement

This book could not have come together without the help of so many people.

First, I have to give the greatest honor to God who has given me the strength and courage to move on with my life. Thanks to my husband and children who have supported me even though at times I was impossible to live with.

A special thanks to my family and friends who continue to surround me with their love and support, as well as their prayers, I'm grateful for every one of you. Also, I want to say a big thanks to Pastor Joanna Birchett and Gospel 4 U Publishing for helping me with the process of publishing this book. I'm so amazed with your gift and commitment to the Lord. I couldn't have done this without you.

To all my readers, thank you all for reading my story.

BEAUTIFUL SOUL

Introduction

This book is written to keep my son's memory alive, it is not easy to lose a love one but even harder when it is your child. In his book I wanted to share with the world the great person my son Esroy was. His life was cut short but I thank God for the great memories that the Lord has allowed me to be able to capture and put into the chapters of this book. As I write each chapter it enables me to move on with my life in a productive manner. It is my prayer that this book bless every reader and that you will see my Esroy for the person that he was. I also hope that my words will encourage any parent that has lost their son or daughter traumatically.

It is my prayer that God will give you the same peace he has given me to continue living my life, knowing that my baby "Esroy" is at peace.

BEAUTIFUL SOUL

ESROY GEORGE ROWE

Foreword

This book is going to share an extraordinary story of a son that was everything to his mother, it's going to show you how awesome this young man was, I thank God for allowing me to be a part of their lives for over fifteen years It was a blessing to watch him grow up into a wonderful young man,

Eileen is a great mother that's why it was very difficult to watch her go through such grief, but in spite of her tragedy and loss of her beautiful son she was thinking about others just as her son would, his purpose here on earth was fulfilled and as he gave in life he gave in death, the only thing I can begin to understand is the courage, the kindness and the compassion it took to extend life to someone else when her loving devoted son was gone. I ask God why he allow such tragedy to happen, many of us turn to God with our anger and disappointment, we talk to God with a one sided conversation, In which we demand answers like why me Lord? Or where were you when I need you? Or what did I do to deserve this? But we know it's our emotions of fear and anger talking because God always says, have faith. Faith is not a feeling, it's not a good luck charm, it's not a higher power who review our wish list and grants or denies our hearts desire, instead faith is a relationship with God, you just have to turn to him he is able to take what is broken and redeem your situation no matter what. When you read this book you will get a better understanding of the true meaning of life and how to forgive and to accept death and most off all how a mother is learning to accept the death of her beloved son. God is able to do exceedingly abundantly anything we could ever ask for. When you read this book it will open up your heart to understanding and forgiveness.

Patericia Vanhoutven
Family Friend and Therpist

Beautiful Soul

BEAUTIFUL SOUL

Chapter 1

This story is about a young boy who had grown into an extraordinary young man, but unfortunately lost his life in a tragic and senseless way, this chapter is an introduction of Esroy George Rowe, life is precious so I encourage you to cherish every moment of every day with your love one.

Ecclesiastes 3:12-*13* ~ *So I concluded there is nothing better than to be happy and enjoy ourselves as long as we can. And people should eat and drink and enjoy the fruits of their labor, for these are gifts from God.*

BIRTH

I knew there would come a time when I would have to say goodbye to my little boy, I just didn't realize that it would happen so soon. Before I became a parent, I was a skinny little teenager going to school and studying to become a teacher. I could not have imagined that a child would bring me so much joy and in the end so much sadness. I know we all must face death someday, but I never thought it would be so soon, and never thought it would be like this. With that being said, I'd like to say to each and every one, live everyday like it is your last. Appreciate the simplest things in your life, cherish your children, treasure every moment with your wife and/or husband, and seize every moment you get with your family and friends because you never know when it is your time to go.

On December 23, 1983, two days before Christmas, Esroy George Rowe graced the world with his presence.

He was born weighing 7 lbs. and was 12 in. long. He was the first child for both of his parents, Eileen Carter (mother) and Albert George Rowe (father). He was born in Jackson Town, Trelawny, Jamaica. Greg, as he was affectionately called by everyone, was a very cute and loveable baby. From the first time you looked at him, you were bound to fall in love. This cuddly baby was our heart beat; we loved him beyond our wildest dreams. He was spoiled by his aunts and uncles and especially his grandmother; love was the apple of her eye, as they would say in Jamaica. As a toddler, he would cry for his mama and didn't want to leave her arms. From such a tender age, we could tell he was going to be very protective of her, and that he was.

He was a very shy kid and never liked to be the center of attention. While taking pictures, his back was always turned towards the camera and his hands were always covering his face. He was just a fun-loving kid. From a very young age I taught him the importance of family; to love your family no matter what, be kind to each other, treat each other with respect as well as having respect for your mother and father and anyone else that you come in encounter with. His grandmother, Una Carter, always told him "Manners will take you over the whole world even without money." And he did listen to her because he was so respectful to everyone that he met. He would melt everyone's heart that he encountered, with his infectious smile. If you were in a bad mood and looked at him with that smile, you would forget about your troubles. You could just tell the kind of person he would grow up to be; you could see it in his walk, his smile, his gentle touch, we just knew he was going to be a very special young man.

BEAUTIFUL SOUL

Chapter 2

Esroy was a teenager who was very enthusiastic about life, in this chapter you will begin to gain access into his teenage years and see how humble and blessed he was. He exhibite pure love and kindness, all the time.

Colossians 3:12 ~ *Therefore, as God's chosen people, holy and dearly loved, clothe yourselves with compassion, kindness, humility, gentleness and patience.*

Teenager

Growing up, Esroy was a very humble kid. Everyone spoiled him, especially his aunts and uncles. He was very active from a tender age; he loved sports. Whatever games you can think of, he was playing. At the age of 11, Esroy migrated to the United States of America with his mother, Eileen; stepfather, Michael; and his sister, Nickeshia, who was four years younger than he was. Coming to the United States was a very big adjustment for him, especially with his Jamaican accent; middle school was a challenge for him. Kids would make fun of him, he was very shy, and because of that, he was being bullied, but the beautiful soul that he had, resulted in him never complaining. He kept on going and taking their beatings until one day he came home crying. I was so mad while listening to him. I sat him down and said "listen to me; you are nobody's beating dummy. If you come home again and tell me those kids beat you up again, I'm going to beat you myself". I also stated that if they hit him, he needs to hit them back. The next day, a group of boys started to beat up on him, and the Jamaican in him came out, and I guess my words were ringing in his ears because he did give it back to them. He took out all six kids by himself; he was sent to the principal's office and was suspended for three days. The best thing that came out of this ordeal was those boys became his friends, and no one ever messed with him ever again.

After elementary, he went on to Olney High School where he did well; he was very involved in all sports, he loved them all. Whatever sports were going on, he was in; especially football, he loved football. One day he said to me "Are you coming to my gymnastic competition?" My mouth dropped I said "What? Gymnastics? Are you crazy, you don't do gymnastic?" He said "I do now" and sure enough he did and loved it. After high school, he went back to assist in coaching the girl's soft ball team. Football was his game, not long after high school, he joined a football team, and he was very good at it. There were several coaches from different colleges that were interested in him. Unfortunately, he did not get to fulfill his dreams because his life was cut short. His dreams were to be a professional football player. He had a lot of potentials, and I know he would have made an excellent football player with a wonderful future.

His teenage year leading up to his adulthood was a very interesting and exciting time for Esroy. He started to get interested in girls as well as girls being interested in him. Oh my! At times it was a competition that I didn't even know I was competing in because they all thought I was his girlfriend. He was so open to me about little things which happened to be very amazing to me, but I was happy that he and I were able to have such an open relationship to where he could talk to me about any and everything. He wasn't afraid of anything nor did he regret anything because he never did anything to have regrets. He always chose his friends carefully and nobody could influence him to do anything he didn't want to do, no matter who was drinking or smoking he wouldn't do it. Even if it were me, he still wouldn't do it; not even a glass of wine with dinner as we always do.

He never gets mad at anyone or anything. He would

always say "I'm more than ordinary, I'm uncommon" and he was so right, he was such a gentle soul. Greg loved his food; he was a lover of bread and ketchup. He would never eat his meals without his bread and his ketchup; he just enjoys eating. He was a strong, healthy teenager; we all know this period in kids life today is not easy, it's the usual conflict between parent and child. I can truly say this time in Esroy's life was one of the happiest we had; video games were his passion at night that was his entertainment. This time in his life he was very focused, I can truly say he was on his way to a bright future. Teenagers don't want to be told what to do or how to do it; they do not want to be cautioned every step of their life, and that's what we tend to do with our children, but I can say that Esroy appreciated me doing that to him. Esroy would obey every word I say; he would do as I say; I would tell him what and how to do it and he would not complain. I often say to him "Greg you can say no" and he would say "Why? You say it mom and I will do it". That is the person that he was.

Traveling was our "thing." Every chance we got, we would go somewhere, whether it was the movies or going to dinner. Greg would eat so fast just so he could look at everyone else eating, so he could make fun of them. Driving to another state or flying to another country was our passion; he used to love spending time with his family. His desire to help people was impeccable; he was fun, loving, and compassionate. He had such an infectious smile; if you were in a bad mood, he knew just what to do to cheer you up. This kid was so strong; I don't know where he got the strength from; he could pick you up and spin you around without breaking a sweat. He was so willing and eager to learn, he was such a good influence on all of his friends and everyone else he would come in contact with. He always tried to motivate them positively; he was a role model for all of them. They all could relate to him one way or another.

These are the things each of his friends would say about him: he is forgiving, he has courage, Esroy has his creativity, he was curious, had empathy, was very fair, had leadership skills, a very generous young man, that was honest, and had love for everyone.

Chapter 3

What do we do when tragedy strikes? Tragedy strikes when we least expect it, life consists hurt and pain but despite it all the pain and hurt, we serve a God that can calm any storm. When we are weak, He is our strength and comfort. When bad things happen as hard as it might seem, we have to let go and let God do what He does, give it all to him.

Psalm 23:4 ~ *"Even though I walk through the valley of the shadow of death, I will fear no evil, for you are with me; your rod and your staff, they comfort me."*

Tragedy

Tragedy strikes when we least expect it to. I never expected it to happen to me; this was so far from my mind that my son who was so young and full of life would have gone so soon. It was October 30, my daughters 18th birthday; it was supposed to be one of the happiest days of our lives. It turned out being the worst night we could have ever imagined. The day started out beautiful, Esroy went to football practice, and my daughter went out to dinner with her friends to celebrate her birthday. I decided to make dinner for the rest of my family. As I was making dinner, Esroy came home and walked into the kitchen with his little sister (Christina), who at the time was two years old, he sat on one of the stools and started playing with her. At that moment, my neighbor started honking his horn from his car and Esroy got up to look through the kitchen window. As he looked, he said " OH NO! I have to move my car; I parked in his driveway" with a smile on his face. "I'll be right back," he said, never knowing that would be the last time I would see him smile.

A couple of hours later, he was gone because his boss called and asked him to do a favor; he asked if Esroy could come into the restaurant because he was short. A group of teenage decided to get into a mischievous night egg tossing. Eventually, this led to one of them pulling out a gun and started shooting inside the restaurant where my son was working. The fearless, kind, and compassionate person that Esroy was, he didn't think about himself. He was getting everyone in the restaurant to safety, especially the kids. Unfortunately for him, the last of the ten bullets that were fired got him in the back of his head. It was 9:15 pm I was upstairs getting ready for bed when I heard someone at the door. My husband was downstairs, so he opened the door, at that moment; a feeling like no other took over my body. I just knew something terrible had happened. As I moved towards the stairs to find out who was at the door, I heard my son's friend, Rohan. I said to him "What's wrong? What's wrong? Where's Greg?" He said, "Come quick, come quick, Esie got shot!" I said "What? Are you crazy?" He said "No, for real. Let's Go!" I was beginning to lose myself. I went tumbling down the stairs, "It's not Greg, It's not him." He said, " You have to put some clothes on, you're in your pj's." "I don't mind, let's go," I said. On our way to the hospital, I was praying "Dear God, PLEASE, PLEASE don't take him away." We pulled up in front of the emergency room door. I jumped out of the car and ran inside screaming "where's my son?" The security guard came over to me trying to calm me down. I told him my son just came in and that he got shot. He told me he would be right back; he left me for a few minutes which felt like forever. He came back and said, "follow me, they took him upstairs." 'Upstairs?" I said, "Wow! That was fast it must not be that bad".

I felt like a burden started to lift off of my shoulder. This has to be good new, we got upstairs, and the guard put us in a waiting room. He told us that someone would be with us shortly which turned into forever. Finally, a gentleman showed up, and without introducing himself, he just asked us has anyone spoke to us yet. We all answered "no." At this time, we were all heated with a look of anger on our faces. I asked what was going on he told us that we could go in and he showed us to his room. I asked him if they did surgery already and he said no and that there would be no surgery taking place because where he got shot, there was nothing that they could do. I said "ok; this is good news. Thank you, God, he's going to be "ok." Without warning or a word of caution, this gentleman walked us into this room where they had my son. I turned to him and asked him "Are you out of your mind? Are you serious right now? Really! A ventilator? Oh my God, you could've at least given us a warning to what we were to expect" I looked at my child hooked up to all kinds of machines, it felt like I was in a scene from a movie. This can't be real. This is not my son, I just turned to the guy who was still standing there and asked "Does this look ok to you? You say it's ok but what is ok with this?" I thought I was going to walk in that room and see my son sitting up in that bed with a big 'ole smile on his face.

By this time, denial began to set in as well as hope. My mind went into overdrive. I'm going to rearrange the house when they release him. I'll take him home and take care of him. He'll be ok. I started talking to God; I said: "Listen now God, it's not his time yet." I held Esroy's hand and said to God "look at him, he's so handsome, he's so young and has his whole life ahead of him. He's a good kid. He doesn't smoke or drink. He is not running wild in these streets. Please, God, don't take him, send him back" I sat at his bedside for hours and nothing, no movements. At this time, I'm thinking how this could have happened I was so numb inside. My world was falling apart around me, and there was nothing I could do to stop it.

I was angry at myself for letting him leave the house; he was not supposed to be at work. He was doing his boss a favor. I was angry at him for leaving the houses and for helping those kids in the restaurant out of danger. I was mad at the doctors because they weren't doing anything to bring him back to me, but the person I was most angry at was God. Why are you taking him away from me? I asked why... Please? The doctors came in and said they are going to run some tests to be sure if there is no brain activity. They asked us to step out the room. I replied saying "step out of the room? What, you all crazy. Any tests that you are going to run, I will be right here". I told them when he opens his eyes I will step out. My son's friend, Rohan encouraged me to take a break. With a lot of persuasions, I decided to leave the room for a bit. I said to my son "you better no go anywhere, I'll be right back. If you can hear me give me a sign" I knew he still in there somewhere and there it was, a tear rolled down his cheek. They took me home for two seconds, and I jumped in the shower (quickest shower ever) put some clean clothes on and said: "let's go."

We got back to the hospital so fast that they didn't even know we were gone. As I entered his room, there was a calm feeling in the atmosphere. I took his hand again and said "I'm back again, " and the tear came rolling down his face, I just know he heard me. He knew I was there and all I could do was say "thank you God he's still here" When the doctors walked in and wanted to talk to us, I was overjoyed because in my heart I felt like they had good news. To my dismay, it wasn't good news. They did five different tests, and none showed any form of brain activity. He said that if there was even a slight movement we could hope. He then continued by saying "At this time, October

31, I pronounce him brain dead". I looked at everyone in the room and said "brain dead, ok that's fine. He's still alive, just the brain, ok no problem I'll take care of him" They all looked at me funny like I was crazy or something. I said "What? He didn't say dead, he said brain dead." In my mind, I believed he would be fine. As he lay there, my heart was heavy and the tears began running down my face. I just heard his voice in my ear saying "you worry too much; everything is going to be ok."

Chapter 4

Esroy's purpose here on earth was fulfilled, what he gave in life, he also gave in death and because of his love for life several people has been blessed with health, hope and the promise of life.

Psalm 138:8 ESV ~ *The Lord will fulfill his purpose for me; your steadfast love, O Lord, endures forever. Do not forsake the work of your hands.*

DONATION

We were all gathered at my son's bedside when all of a sudden one of the machines started to beep. Instantly, a lady showed up, and at that time I didn't know who she was until later when I was told that she was one of the ladies from the gift of life foundation. She came in really mad because apparently his body temperature has dropped and no one noticed. They put an electric blanket on him and started to warm his body, and when I saw this, I began having hope again. I began thinking that the doctors were wrong, but no such luck a few minutes later the same lady came back in the room to have a meeting with my family and me about the situation and where we would go from here. We followed her into a private room where we were met by two other people. They were also from the gift of life foundation, and they wanted to know what I think about organ donation. They wanted to know if I would be interested in donating my son's organs. I replied saying "Yes if he were dead because my son loves people and he loves life, but he's not dead." They all looked at me funny as to say he's dead. My friend Philomena who was there turned to me and said: "he's dead."

She continued to speak, and I said to her "Phil, no he's not dead...his brain is, but his body isn't."

She said "Eileen brain dead means dead."

I replied saying "No, brain dead means brain dead, go look at his heart it is still beating, that means his body is still alive."

"Yes, but he can't live without his brain," she said.

One of the ladies turned to me, and she said to me "Yes, you are right. His body is still alive, and his organs are still alive, but it's the machines that are breathing for him. You can keep him on the machines for as long as you want but he's not going to have a productive life. Life, as we know it for him, is over. His organs are going to start shutting down then. Eventually, he's going to die."

At that moment, I realized I only wanted him to live for me because I can't live without him. I can't live in this world knowing he's not in it but I realized it's not fair to him. The young man we all have known and loved would not want to live like this. He was always going somewhere and doing something enjoying life. At that moment, I decided to let his physical body go and let his organs live in someone else's body, so I decided on the donation. I was waiting for my brother, Michael, and his family to come in from Canada to spend time with him. They told me to take as much time as I wanted with him.

"it might not be now, it might not be today, it might not be tomorrow, but I will," I replied

I went back into his room where by this time a lot of friends and family are gathering crying and hugging each other. I look up at the machine watching the steady beat of his heart. I touched his hand, and it felt so warm, so soft. If only you were just sleeping, I kissed his forehead; I smelled his hair, I constructed a memory of him to carry with me at all times. I whispered "Goodbye my son; I love you I promised I would keep your memories alive. Son you will live on." This precious heart I'm looking at beating is going to live on. I know at the moment he was smiling down at me.

Finally, my brother and his family arrived; doubt and fear

set in again when he said he's not dead. It was a very difficult decision for my brother to let go because he loved him like his own. I watched him say his goodbyes which were very painful, and I decided to sign the papers to donate his organs. At that moment a feeling of peace took over me, and I knew I was doing the right thing because his beautiful heart will live on. He is still alive, not in his body, but in someone else's. We were all just standing around in the hallway talking, crying, and wondering if we did the right thing; wondering if the doctors could have done something more, asking God why. Should we have waited? Should we have asked for more testing? Then all of a sudden, there he was behind us. They were taking him down the OR for surgery. That instant I lost it, I held on to the bed saying "NO, NO, NO. I change my mind; I can't let you guys do this. I want him back please, please!" They did not listen to me. They didn't even stop. That made me so angry. This was the hardest thing I ever had to do in my life, and I hope I don't ever have to do it again.

If anyone reading this book has ever lost a child, you all have an idea of the pain I'm talking about. It's like a part of your soul is gone. If you have never lost a child, you can not begin to understand my pain. Just try and put your feet in my shoes and wear it for a day then maybe, just maybe you will understand what I'm going through. People at times would ask "how you doing?" with a smile. I would reply saying "ok," but that wasn't true because how should I be doing? I don't know. Some would say "he's gone already, there's nothing you can do so move on." How can I move on?, move on to what?, move on to where ? if they only know it's the grace of God surrounding me. It's his grace that sustains me, and his mercy that gives me the will power to go on. I take each steps day by day, I know he will not leave me neither for sake me, he is walking beside me each day; when I slip he is always behind me to hold me up. I know that my handsome, talented, and beautiful son is at peace resting in God's loving hands.

Esroy was one of the best souls you could ever meet, so when I was watching the steady beat of his heart, I knew I had to keep it alive. When the gift of life organization reached out to me about the donation, I had to say yes. After eight years of my son's death, I started to feel guilty about giving away his organs. Everyday I think about the four people that his organs have saved. I question myself and wonder if I did the right thing. After that tragic night, apart from the letter that was sent to me, I never heard from the organization again nor any of the recipients or their families. I didn't ask for any recognition, profit, or fame but when I think about the lives he saved and families he put back together, I have to wonder were these people grateful. No one, I mean no one, showed any form of appreciation. I'm very disappointed that none of these people took the time out to find out where their gifts came from. It pains my heart to know that I gave away part of my son to people that didn't realize the gift I had given them.

I just pray and hope that one day they will acknowledge that I have given them something so special, the most precious thing in the world. It's just sad for me when I heard other recipients talk about their gift that they have received and I was thinking, what about me? I would give anything just to hear my son's heart beat. My son's brain died, not his heart. So my belief is he is still alive somewhere out there, and it pains me just thinking about it.

Yes, I know people out there are saying "you could contact them." But why would I contact them? I don't know you; you don't know me. You don't want to know who gives you such a precious gift come on now. I just prayed and hoped that that they are taking very good care of themselves and that they will have a happy and healthy life. I'm trying so very hard to understand the reluctance of these recipient, its very hard knowing that a part of my son is out here somewhere.

When I lost my son, my whole world fell apart. We didn't have time to say our goodbyes, words for words to each other. I was overwhelmed with sadness. My life changed in the blink of an eye. Holidays are going to be different, at times I feel guilty and angry, but I thank god for faithful friends and family. May my tears of sorrow be tears of joy for the recipient that received my son's gifts. I can just hope and pray that they are grateful. I try and set my mood positively every morning because I want to start my day with a smile. I have my son to thank for that being his mom is the best gift I have ever been given, not even death can take that away.

Chapter 5

When God has a plan for your life there's no one or nothing that can stand in his way, he gives life and he takes it away, Blessed is the name of the Lord. God is a miracle worker and he can turn things around, just like that, our lives is in his hands.

Jeremiah 29:11 (NIV) ~ *For I know the plans I have for you," declares the LORD, "plans to prosper you and not to harm you, plans to give you hope and a future.*

A Miracle

One year and three months into Esroy's death, God gave me a gift beyond my wildest dreams. I started having cramps in my stomach so bad that I went to the doctor and I began explaining the issue to her. She asked me if I thought I was pregnant and I laughed while responding "most definitely not."

She said "ok; we will find out."

She did the urine test, and it showed up negative, with a laugh again, I said: "I told you so." She said, "well I guess you aren't, you're just late." She sent me home with a year's worth of birth control pills saying "you can start taking it tonight it will be ok." I went home and decided not to take them because I still didn't like how I was feeling. I went back to her, and she did another urine test. It came up negative again. She said "ok; we are going to do a blood test because whatever is in the blood, it will show up." She told me she would call me the next day with the results. Whatever it was, the next day came, and I heard nothing from the doctor. The following day still nothing until I forgot about the test because I was feeling better.

Finally, the fourth day came, and I got a call from my doctor. She was like "I thought you were just stressed from losing your son, but it's not" I replied saying "If it's not stress and I'm not going crazy then what is it?" With a laugh, she said "well it's my time to laugh. Congratulations you are pregnant "No way, you must be crazy, this cannot be real" With a laugh again, she said "yes way, come in tomorrow, and we will see how far along you are" I went home and called a family meeting to inform everyone about the test results. You would've thought we had won the lottery the way they were jumping up and down saying "It's Greg! It's Greg!"

My pregnancy was very bad, I ended up in the hospital many times, but thanks be to God I had a safe delivery and a healthy baby boy. We named him Michael, and it felt like Deja Vu, Michael's features were just like Greg. He was born on October 31st on the second anniversary of Esroy's death. His due date was supposed to be on November 12th, but by some miracle, he was here on the same tragic date. As we all know, God makes no mistakes. He took one and gave me one for whatever reason. I'm grateful; I guess he knows my heart, he knew I would not be able to go on. He put one back to help me along the way. God is such an amazing God. About a year later I realized that my due date was on November 12th which happens to be the same date I buried Esroy. He was supposed to be born to keep me from falling to pieces, everything about this child reminds me of Esroy. He plays like him, jokes like him, likes video game and football like him, and even likes ketchup on everything just like

Esroy.

Every little thing he does brings me joy and a sense of peace because he reminded me of Esroy so much. His memory will never die. So when I'm feeling sad and depressed, I just have to look at Michael. There is a lot of empty yesterdays and will always be a lot of empty tomorrows, so for right now we have to cherish every single moment, and we live life to the fullest. Don't take one single moment for granted. Enjoy your children while you still can because you never know when you or they will take your last breath.

 Grief is a very confusing and unpredictable and honestly very difficult for everyone. It's been a long road and will continue to be. God is walking me through; this grief has no time limit, and you will never stop grieving it just gets a little easier to cope with. I know I have to move on with my life because I know Esroy would not want me to be stuck in a depressive state.

He would want me to live life to the fullest. He would often say "you worry too much, you going to get gray hair before you get old." I would reply saying "don't get into trouble because, my heart, I can't take it."
In response, he would say "your heart is stronger than you think." So with his words in my head all the time, reminding me one day at a time and one step at a time sometimes even one minute at a time. God's grace and mercy will see me through.

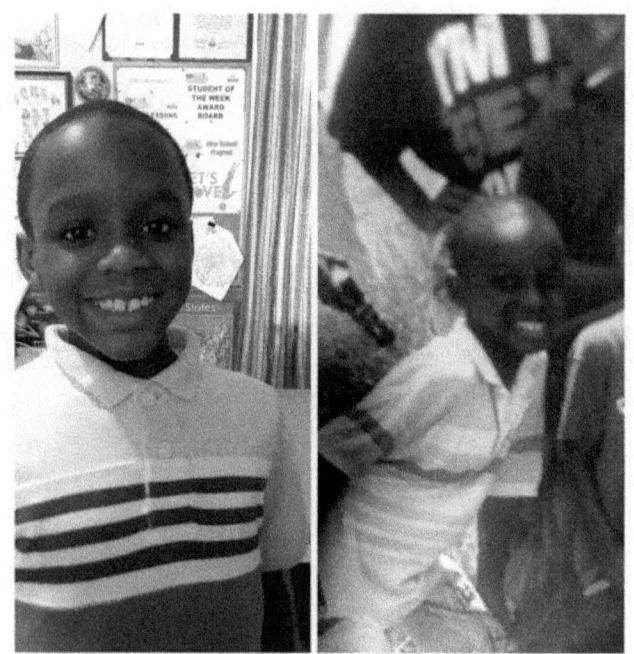

Michael & Esroy

Chapter 6

The waiting period has ended, its now time for justice to be served, but disappointment is beginning to try to take away our peace, but in the end, God stepped in and justice was served, and the Lord gave us peace. My son's soul is at rest, and now we can all move on with our lives.

Philippians 4:7 ~ *And the peace of God, which transcends all understanding, will guard your hearts and your minds in Christ Jesus.*

TRIAL

The trial started instantly. The guy turned himself in and pleaded guilty, so everything was straight forward. The arraignment date was February 1, 2006, after that, the trial date was set and things was going accordingly and then wow he change his plea to not guilty, he got himself a lawyer and decided he's innocent. (I bet you could only imagine my anger). Now he wanted to plea innocent and said he didn't do it. I wanted to kill him with my bare hands. Four months later, we went back to court for the status hearing. At the time, I didn't know what this hearing was about, but I came to find out that it was to keep the judge up to date; as to their progress towards the trial. To top it off, they informed me that this hearing could last over a period of 6-9 months. We did not get another hearing date until

October of 2006, which was rescheduled as the date got closer, the next date was a year later sometime in 2007. The time after that was in January of 2008 where they came up with a false confession, and they continue the hearing to see if he was competent to stand trial.

They got their hearing another year later in February of 2009, and they did find him competent to withstand the trial. The pre-trial date was set for another year later. They offered him a plea deal and eventually years went the past, and still, nothing was getting accomplished. I thought this thing would never end. I did a lot of phones calling in between these months and shed a lot of tears from frustration wondering when this was going to end. I couldn't understand why it was taking so long; they got the guy, and he confessed so why is it taking years to be done with? My son is gone. To take him for no reason, he didn't know you, and you didn't know him so why not tell the truth?

In February of 2013, I got a call from the D.A. office, and they said that we finally have a date. I screamed on the phone "it's about time." Unfortunately, it got put off again, and I was so fed up with these people and the court system.

This time I was spitting fire because the guy killed my son and no one seems to care. I went down on my knees, and I asked God why. Why God? "I'm still waiting for your answer. You let this thug take his life, and now you are not doing anything to let him pay for it?" I didn't know what to do at this point, but I remember someone once said, "when trial and tribulations bring you to your knees you are in the perfect position to pray" so I got down on my knees, and I prayed. I prayed that God would give me the strength to go on. I let it go and said, "God it's all in your hands."

Another year passed, and nothing happened. Finally, in

February of 2015, I got a call from the D.A. again (laughing) she said: "Mrs. Carter he took the deal, He's pleading guilty." I told her that we were right back where we started ten years, but to God be the glory, we're getting somewhere. We got a trial date with the judge for April, the disappointment set in again because they changed the date. I began to remember as my pastor Bishop Shawn Bartley would say: "when you know that God got you, you don't have to fight the battle alone. Just let go and let him do the rest." He said "just invite God into your circumstances no matter what it is." I really applied those words to my thoughts. They changed it again but I said "Lord, I leave it in your hands." This is my storm that I am going through and I won't come out bitter, I am coming out better. I have to for my son's sake. Finally, we got a date, this was it. We still had our fingers crossed but it wasn't. I didn't know how to feel; the day has finally come.

It has been nine years, seven months and nine days since my son was taken away from me. How am I supposed to feel? I don't know. Have you ever loved someone so deep inside that when they are gone forever its hard for you to get them off your mind? Have you ever cried so much that it hurt to even move, it felt like your heart is coming out your chest? Have you ever told someone that you were ok knowing that you were really lying? That was me. For such a long time I have felt so alone. With tears running down my face I watch as they escort this young man into the court room, all my emotion came flooding in, but at the same time. I have to compose myself, and control my thought, this is the person who has taken away my son from me his dad, his sisters and brothers, his family and friends, all have to hear him say." I did it, I killed Esroy George Rowe" and I want him to explain why he did it. The judge asked him to stand and state his name. she then proceeded to explain the situation to him, she asked him, do you understand? And he answered by saying, yes ma'am.

She asked him "how do you plea?"

"Guilty" he replied

"Why?" she said.

'I don't know" he said.

"You know why, tell his mother why," said the judge

"I was stupid and showing off. I got the gun from my friend. I am so sorry from the bottom of my heart. I know I can not bring Esroy back but he is asking for our forgiveness." As I sat there listening to him, my heart bleeds for him. As I think about forgiving him I can hear my brother Michael saying "Don't do it, I know you. You are too forgiving; remember he took away your son." But I have to make a choice to give up my desire of revenge. I have to show compassion and forgiveness. I will never forget or excuse what he did, but I have to substitute my negative with positive feelings and thoughts.

When the judge handed down his ruling, our mouths dropped. She sentenced him to 28 years without parole, 10 of which he already did, so initially he's only doing 18 more. It was sad, sad, sad, I didn't get justice the way I wanted it but I did get closure. My only hope is that he comes out a changed man like he said he would. I also hope that he'll be an asset to society by living a clean and honest life. As the trial came to an end, he stood with his family behind him and he didn't turn around to look at them but as he made his way out of the room, he turned around with a quick glance our eyes connected and at that time I could tell that he was truly sorry.

This was such a sad day, for 9 years and 7 months, I suffered immensely, the anticipation was killing me slowly. It was such a sad day, this was such a senseless killing. A part of me has been taken away form me that I can never ever get back. My heart ached so deeply with sadness, but today I can breathe a little better knowing that he's taking responsibility for his actions. The loss of my child is a grief that will last forever but at least I can try and move on from now on. I will try to forgive but I will never ever forget. I truly believe that if I don't allow myself to forgive I will be setting myself up for a lifetime of pain. Forgiveness feels better than holding onto the hate, it's hard to let go but I will and I am.

Chapter 7

The day has come for our final goodbyes, this was the hardest day of my life, I pray that I would never have to endure this type of trauma again.

I'm walking in faith with God's hands wrapped around me, he is ordering my steps and he spoke these words in my spirit, *"All things works together for good"* I know I will be ok. Rest my son you are in God's loving arms.

Romans 8:28 ~ *And we know that all things work together for good to them that love God, to them who are the called according to his purpose.*

BEAUTIFUL SOUL

THE FUNERAL

The day has come for us to say our goodbye's our old world has come to a standstill, saying goodbye to someone that you least expect to die has changed our lives forever ,Numbness sets in, oh my God this is a day you don't want to go through, so many people tried to cheer me up with kind encouraging words, but I didn't want to hear it, not today, I was so out of control, I could not control my emotions, fear began to try and overtake me, I start thinking it's so dark, in that hole, he's going to be alone now, it was so difficult just thinking about it, at one point I could not speak I was just praying in my spirit , just asking God to strengthen me ,to give me the will power to get through the ordeal, I don't know how to do this, we had two memorial services, one here in Philadelphia where he lived and one in Jackson Town Trelawney in Jamaica where he was born and raised for the first 11 years of his life. The first funeral day came and o my world God give me the strength to get through this day, because without you God I can't do it I plan this service in a daze I think I was in another world I never expect to bury my child, I didn't have a plan I have no idea on what to do but I have to face it, everyone wanted to do the arrangement for me, but I said no, I needed to do it myself, I brought him in this world and I am going to send him home, I know I was sitting in the church don't know how I got there or who was there or even what was been said but with God's help I made it through. I flew his body back to Jamaica for burial, the morning of was the worst day of my life, this was it, once we put him under he is no more.

No one had slept the night before people were coming from all over around 7 o'clock in the morning we heard this loud bawling around the grave sight, we all run over to see what's going on to my surprise it was my older brother Michael, he was down in the grave crying uncontrollably he was not coming out of this grave because no one was going to put his nephew in there !it takes an hour and four guys to go down in the hole to get him out that just break my heart all over again .just to see the out pouring of love showed me how much he is loved. I sleep walk through this final memorial service. I lost it when they lower his body down I will never see my son again, someone walk me away from the grave sight at that moment I could feel my head spinning in circles, I don't remember what happened afterwards, but I woke up to a voice saying it will be ok God got you! I know that was the voice of my amazing son.

Life Goes On
"Words from Author"

Comfort me with your love oh God, calm my fearful heart, wrap me up in your arms. for all my hope begins with you. Is it true what they say when a child is born a mother's heart is no longer her own? It runs and skips, it giggles and grins, it crawls in her lap for a kiss on the cheek, but where goes her heart when that child is gone? is it true that life goes on? Does the passage of time means it should make sense? can loss be measured in time? As I yearn for the day when I'll see my son again.

It has been said that life goes on, but being saved I understand it better, according to 2 Cor. 5:8 *"We are confident, I say, and willing rather to be absent from the body, and to be present with the Lord.*

I will not question God, but I am still trying to figure out why? Why I will never see you again? But one thing I know is that God is Jehovah Shalom, He is my peace and I am at peace. Thank you Jesus! I can see your beautiful smile in the beam of the sun, the twinkling of your eyes now shines, I hear your laugh in the lyrics of songs that you always sing, it is strange to think that your heart still beats inside some stranger whom I will never get to meet, does she knows she carries a heart of gold from my sweet baby boy who will never grow old, so many lives saved by your own, it leaves me to believe that life does goes on.

Letters From Families & Friends

BEAUTIFUL SOUL

Letter From Aunt Pat

Gone too soon are the only that I can find right now to describe how much I have missed this remarkable, honest, caring, talented and fun loving young man.

He was such a positive big brother, a best friend, a son who many mother's envy. whether biological or otherwise. From a young age we knew he had great potential to be the best. Greg always thrives to be perfect, he carriers all these qualities with him.

In his life as a young adult. there has never been a day when we don't have a fond memory of him. Greg was full of life, he had a passion for food, he loved a good Jamaican hard dough bread, Greg had the biggest most beautiful smile, he was full of respect he was certainly a role model. There's not enough words to tell you today how much we miss him .apart of us went with him when he dies, today my greatest regret is on that

BEAUTIFUL SOUL

sad day why didn't someone stop the evil act, we are left with so much beautiful memories of you. God has another angel in heaven looking down on us. I know you are safe in his loving arms.
LOVE YOU ENDLESSLY MY NEPHEW, REST IN PEACE.

Letter From Grandma

To my dear grandson,

I still can't believe you are gone. I miss that big beautiful smile of yours, I thank God for the wonderful memories we have made, I delivered you from your mother's womb, I was the first one to welcome you into this world, from the first time I laid my eyes on you I knew you were my sunshine, you make me so happy I only hope you know how much I love you,

I know you are smiling down on us, but I just wish that I truly wish that could see those pearly white teeth smiling down on us. I miss you endlessly my boy sleep on until we meet again

Love grandma Una Carter

Letter From Aunt Chincy

My dear Greg

How can I say goodbye. I still can't believe you are gone you were the best son a mother could have ask for, you were the best brother ever and you were the best friend any and everyone would have wish to have ,and last but not least you were the best nephew any auntie would like to have. I miss that smile I miss that warm loving feeling when I'm around you, I'm so happy i was in your life and got to watch you grow into the beautiful young man you have become, sleep on love until we meet again.

from your Auntie Chincy love always

Letter From Your Dad

Greg

Words can't express the pain I'm feeling this is unbelievable, in my wildest dreams I can not imagine you not hear but I guess God has a better plan for you I miss you dearly you will always be in my heart ,thanks for the memories I will surely keep them alive keep on smiling my son

Your Daddy

Letter From Your Mom

My Beautiful Son

How I miss you so, I miss that warm feeling I get from you, Esroy you were more than a son to me, you were my confidant my friend, my inspiration my everything. I hate to see you go, its so lonely without you in my life, every day its a struggle just knowing you are not around.

 I will never understand why God took you from me, but I trust him, I guess he has bigger and better things for you to do. Son you were a priceless gift and I'm so happy that you were mine. I miss that big beautiful smile. I know you are looking down me

Love you much Mom

Letter From Your Stepdad Michael Sr.

Greg,

Saying goodbye is very difficult, it's so sad to see you go, never thought you would leave this soon you were not my biological child but you were no less my son
I was there when you were born, I watched you grow up into this spectacular young man that you were, we all miss you terribly you carry yourself with such grace you were a roll model to all around you i miss you terrible im so proud to call you my son
Stepdad Michael Sr.

Letter From Uncle Michael

Greg

I cant believed you are gone that quick without warning, you are truly missed nephew, words cannot begin to express the feeling that is inside, you were more than a nephew to me, you were one of my sons. You are gone but you will never be forgotten keep on smiling God has a beautiful soul up there with him in Glory
Love you my son
Uncle Michael

Letter From Michael Jr

Greg

I never get to meet you, you were gone before I was born but I heard the great stories about you, how kind and humble you were, fun loving and sweet. Everyone loves you so much and I wished I had the opportunity to meet you. I know we would have been best friend and I hope to grow up and be just like you. I love you.
Your little brother Michael Jr

Letter From Sisters Nickeshia & Christina and Brother Christopher

Our Brother Greg

We miss you so much, you were the best role model ever, you were our dad our brother our friend there will never be another brother like you, we still can't believe you're gone, thanks for the hugs and laughter that we shared, every moment we share will forever be in our hearts. Continue Smiling. We miss you and love you forever, you will never be forgotten.

Sisters Nickeshia & Christina

Brother Christopher

Letter From Aunty Hyacinth

Greg,

I miss you dearly. But I know God got you, I never thought I would be saying goodbye to you so soon I will miss your cheerful attitude we will always remember your smile ,you were a inspirational to everyone you meet you have taught me so much you always say don't let life get you down rise above it, appreciate life keep a smile on your face at all times, everyone will always remember you because of your smile, I will always keep your memories alive.

Love you endlessly

Your Auntie Hyacinth

Letter From Rohan

Ezzi,

We all know life isn't fair, but my question is, Why you? I always say that you were the one that kept us focused, you were the humble one. I started living my life differently because of you, this is not goodbye, we'll meet again You are my boy for life .

Love, Rohan

Letter From Blue Mountain Family

Greg

Words can not express the pain we felt when we lost you, we'll cherish your memories always you will forever live on in our hearts

Blue Mountain Cafe Family

Letter From Your Aunts Jennifer, Joy, Marva

Greg

You were the best of the best, very unique, we never thought we would be saying goodbye to you so soon. We miss you like crazy, God has another angel looking down on us, we love you always keep on smiling

Your Aunt's

Jennifer, Joy, Marva

Letter From Auntie Sandra and Auntie Philomenia

Greg

We Love you dearly and miss you terribly until we meet again keep on smiling.

Letter From Juanita Slowely

As the years have gone by I have watch Esroy exceeded beyond my wildest dreams, he has expanded his personal challenge, he had turn into a wonderful young man he had over come many challenges with optimism. Esroy was certainly one of those people who has made the world a better place, also those lives he has touched, I'm sure that the life Esroy led has given his mother the insight to share his story with you all, whoever read this book will have a chance to experience Esroy generosity and love for those he has left behind.

I thank God every day for the time I have spent with him. I was so overwhelmed by his sudden death I did not know what to do, but when I think back over his life it warms my heart to know that he was an extraordinary person and it was a pleasure having him in my life.

Juanita Slowely

POEMS FROM THE HEART

The loss of a loved one

The loss of a loved one is so hard to face
you just want to hide, go somewhere and escape,
but death is something we all must go through, I know
it's hard especially when it's someone that you love.
But .just know that they are in a better place
no more hurt no more pain shall they face.
It seems unfair but yes this is true,
they are in heaven now watching over me and you.
God has call him home to rest and he's being well
taken care of because God knows best.
I still can't believe that you've gone so soon leaving
behind just memories of you,
but as they say God knows best .
You are always in my heart because in there you're
still alive, losing you creates an emptiness that echoes
every day but I must somehow find the will to carry
on, because as they say God knows best.

Please don't cry

Please don't cry I'm not really gone when you look out
the window I'll be standing on the lawn,
please don't cry I'll see you again,
please don't cry I'm not really dead,
when you cry yourself to sleep
I'll be by your bed, please don't cry just because we
had to part, as long as you remember me
I'll live in your heart.
Please don't cry I'm not gone forever, when you need a
shoulder to lean on I'll be by your side, please don't cry
when you are sad I'll be there to kiss you on the cheek.
Please don't cry this is not a goodbye,
it's until we meet again.

STAY HUMBLE

Humble people are quick to repent when they do something wrong, and that was Esroy, humble people always apologize if they have hurt or offended someone and that was Esroy, They are willing to listen to reason and seriously consider the opinions of others, truly humble people are not rude because they value other people and that was Esroy, they realize other people are equally as valuable as they are, truly humble people give credit to God and others who help them get to where they are.
Humble people show appreciation by taking the time to thank others.

Humility is needed in order to serve others with the right motive and good attitude.
And that was my Son ESROY.

FAITH

When your loved one dies you have to hold on to your faith,
death is one of life's ultimate mystery because it's so difficult to imagine your love one gone forever whether you think death is the end, or a period, or the doorway to life forever it's still hard,
so hold on to your faith.
Faith is believing in things we cannot see, we cannot change our pass, but our decision can affect our present, trust God and he will direct your future, hold on to your faith it will see you through the difficult period in your life,

I'm an overcomer,
I'm a conquer just because
I have Faith.

God gave him to me

From heaven he was delivered as a baby unto me, when God said to me softly I'm trusting you to do everything that's needed to nurture him, he's your little angel sent from me above,
Spirits cannot be held, hugged, or kissed the body that was his vessel is what you will surely miss but his spirit that I shared with you that is what I promised to never take away.
He's back in heaven now the earth was not his place ,he taught you all about dignity and grace ,so as you weep and grieve to see him once again I promise he will be waiting when you get there.

ONE MORE DAY

A thousand words won't bring you back,
I know because I tried, neither will a thousand tears
I know because I've cried.
I wish for nothing more than just one more day,
I would give it all just to hear say
I LOVE YOU

A Child Never Forgotten

Our hearts was broken, without a warning
You were taking away from me someone say you could not stay,
empty and lonely is what I am,
I lost a precious shining star our family torn apart.
Your world began with a promising start but ended with a broken heart,
life is unfair this difficult cross we must bear,
strength and courage we will find our special child always in our mind.
a place in heaven is where you sit,
you will forever be in our hearts, you will never be forgotten my child.

HERE I STAND

Here I stand year after year at your grave side still
trying to accept the decision God made, to take
you home,
I drive myself crazy for a hint or a clue of why at
twenty two he had to take you from me?
He didn't give me a choice to choose you or me, but
obviously God doesn't work like that forever reason he
wanted you that day,
I guess I will never know,
now here I stand with tears in my eyes everyday for
the past years. I can't tell you goodbye, I can only say
I love you. I just wish I could hear your voice, feel
your touch or see your handsome face,
if I lived to see a hundred,
I will still ask him, why?

OPPORTUNITY

Time goes by so fast,
people go in and out of your life,
you must never miss the opportunity to tell these people how much they mean to you.
Give people a chance to restore, renew, revive, reclaim and redeem themselves.
Never throw anyone out of your life.
The greatness of a man is not in how much wealth he acquires but it's his integrity and his ability to affect those around him positively.
Choose to love rather than hate, choose to laugh rather than cry, create than destroy, give than take, pray than curse choose to live than die.
Love the people God gave you because he's going to want them back one day.

Gallery of Memories

BEAUTIFUL SOUL

ESROY "GREG" ROWE

BEAUTIFUL SOUL

BEAUTIFUL SOUL

BEAUTIFUL SOUL

BEAUTIFUL SOUL

BEAUTIFUL SOUL

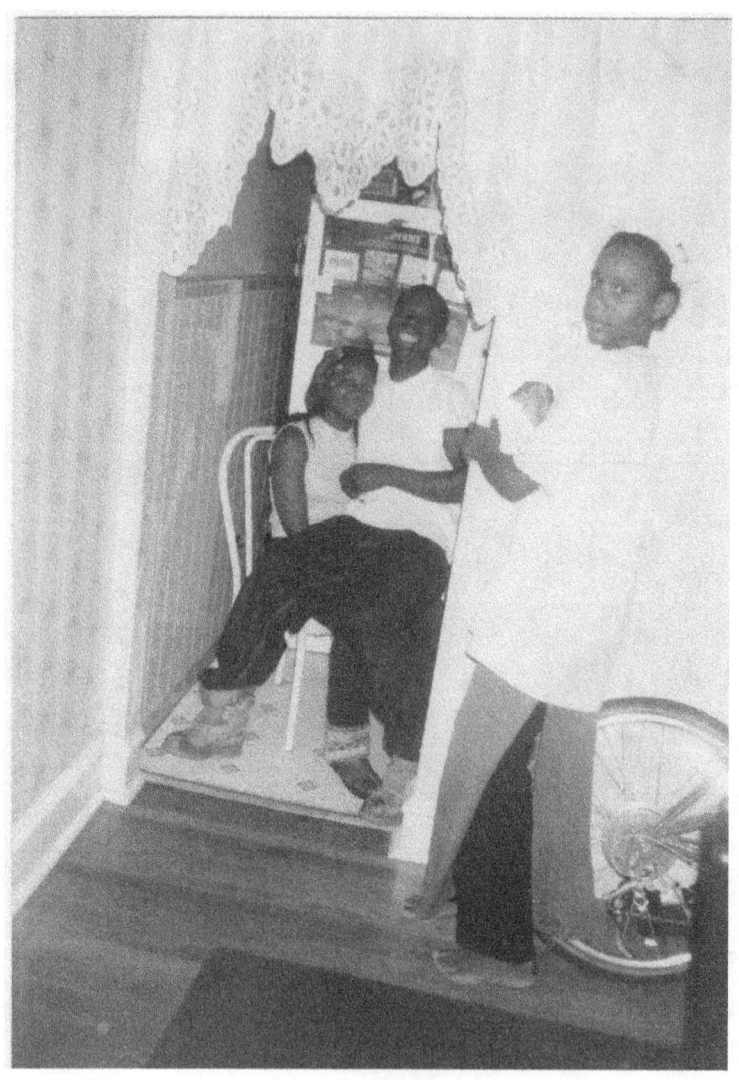

BEAUTIFUL SOUL

Words of Encouragement

Extreme pain—terrible loss—indescribable suffering! These are just a few of the feelings and emotions felt by parents who have lost a child. Obviously, there is nothing that can alleviate that pain except for consolation from the Lord, the love of family and friends, and the passing of time. The Bible says He will never give us more than we can bear, so I encourage you to stand on this. He values His Word above His name.

God's word is a comfort to us during times of terrible grief and mourning.

God not only sympathizes with us when we suffer, but he also empathizes with us as well. His son died on the cross for our sins. So his love for us has an incredible way of turning things around on our behalf.

Where there is grief and loss, God brings soothing and relief.

Where there is pain and suffering, he brings peace and hope.

Only he can turn our mourning into dancing and clothe us with gladness instead of despair during our darkest hours.

As I leave these comforting scriptures that helped me through my days? Allow them to permeate your heart and bring a sense of peace in your life.

Here are my top seven (7) comforting Bible verses for those who have lost a child:

Scriptures

1. *Psalm 30:11 "You have turned for me my mourning into dancing; you have loosed my sackcloth and clothed me with gladness..."*

2. *Isaiah 61:3 "...to grant to those who mourn in Zion— to give them a beautiful headdress instead of ashes, the oil of gladness instead of mourning, the garment of praise instead of a faint spirit; that they may be called oaks of righteousness, the planting of the Lord, that he may be glorified."*

3. *Psalm 23:4 "Even though I walk through the valley of the shadow of death, I will fear no evil, for you are with me; your rod and your staff, they comfort me."*

4. *Matthew 5:4 "Blessed are those who mourn, for they shall be comforted."*

5. *Revelation 21:4 "He will wipe every tear from their eyes. There will be no more death' or*

mourning or crying or pain, for the old order of things has passed away."

6. 2 Corinthians 4:17-18 *"For our light and momentary troubles are achieving for us an eternal glory that far outweighs them all. So we fix our eyes not on what is seen, but on what is unseen, since what is seen is temporary, but what is unseen is eternal."*

7. Isaiah 41:10 *"So do not fear, for I am with you; do not be dismayed, for I am your God. I will strengthen you and help you. I will uphold you with my righteous right hand."*

It might seem impossible for the extreme sadness and grief we feel at the loss of a child to ever diminish or decrease; however, the Lord is our hope and our salvation, and he can turn our mourning into comfort. God wants to encourage us and relieve our suffering if we will just go to him at all times. And his word is powerful enough to bring healing and solace even during our darkest hours.

BEAUTIFUL SOUL

ABOUT THE AUTHOR

Eileen is a Jamaican native, but she has lived in Philadelphia for over twenty years, after her son's death she started a memorial scholarship foundation in his name in Jamaica, she provides school supplies and monetary award to a qualified student each year, this has given her so much joy and it keeps his memory alive.

www.ingramcontent.com/pod-product-compliance
Lightning Source LLC
Chambersburg PA
CBHW070920160426
43193CB00011B/1538